DIGGING UP THE PAST

BODIES *from*
the PAST

ROBIN PLACE

Thomson Learning • New York

DIGGING UP THE PAST

Biblical Sites • Bodies from the Past • Pompeii and Herculaneum • The Search for Dinosaurs • Troy and Knossos • The Valley of the Kings

Cover background: The well-preserved body of the Domlandsmoor girl was found in a bog in Germany. She had been buried there for over two thousand years. (See page 23.)

Cover inset: The magnificent jade burial suit of Tou Wan was one of many treasures found in a tomb near Beijing, China. (See pages 25–27.)

Title page: Tollund Man is one of the most famous "bog bodies" found in Northern Europe. (See pages 21 and 24.)

First published in the United States in 1995 by
Thomson Learning
New York, NY

U.S. copyright © 1995 Thomson Learning

U.K. copyright © 1995 Wayland (Publishers) Ltd

Library of Congress Cataloging in Publication Data
Place, Robin.
　　Bodies from the past / Robin Place.
　　　　p.　　cm.—(Digging up the past)
　　Includes bibliographic references (p.　　) and index.
　　ISBN 1-56847-397-4
　　1. Human remains (Archaeology)—Juvenile
literature. 2. Burial—Juvenile literature. I. Title.
II. Series: Digging up the past (New York, N.Y.)
CC77.B8P58　　1995
930.1028'2—dc20　　　　　　　　95-16426

Printed in Italy

Picture acknowledgments
The publishers would like to thank the following for allowing their photographs to be reproduced in this book: C. M. Dixon 7 (top) (British Museum), 8, 18 (National Museum, Copenhagen); Werner Forman 21 (Silkeborg Museum), 31 (top) (David Bernstein Collection, New York); Robert Harding Picture Library cover (both), 22, 23 (C. Gascoigne), 26, 27; Peter Hicks 29; Hulton Deutsch Collection Ltd. 39; Anton Koler 4; Manchester Museum 14, 16, 17 (left); Herbert Maurer 10 (both); National Museum, Copenhagen 7 (bottom), 19, 20; Natural History Museum, London 33 (Peabody Museum Papers), 34–35 (Bureau of American Ethnology), 36–38; Romisch-Germanisches Zentralmuseum, Mainz 12 (both) (C. Beeck); Rex Features Ltd. 9, 13; Science Photos Ltd. 15 (both) (A. Tsiaras), 28 (R. Ressmeyer); Topham Picture Library *title page*, 5, 24, 41–43; Jerry Young 17 (right). Artwork on page 11 is by Tony Smith. All other artwork is by Peter Bull.

Contents

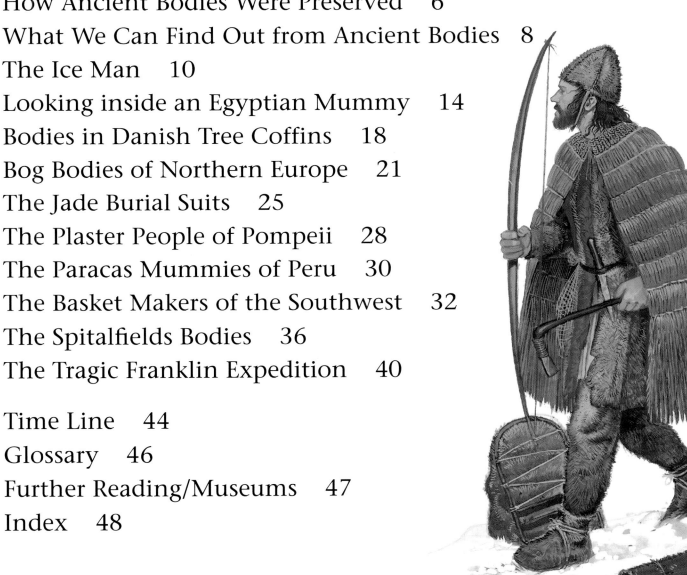

Finding a Body from the Past

The Ice Man of the Alps

In 1991, Helmut Simon and his wife Erika went on vacation to the Tyrol, in Austria, to walk in the mountains. On September 19, the weather was so fine they climbed to the top of a mountain. On the way down, they left the marked path and went toward a rocky gully filled with ice. Suddenly they spotted something sticking out of the ice. It looked like a big doll. Then Erika gasped, "It's a man!"

It was a man, and Helmut thought it must be the body of someone lost in the mountains in recent years. Helmut had just one picture left in his camera, so he took a photograph of the body.

But it was not a modern body—the Ice Man, as he was called, had been lost in the mountains five thousand years ago. It was fortunate that Erika and Helmut found the body when the sun had melted the ice and revealed the upper part of the body. Only three days later, the first winter snow fell, and the body would have been covered up again and perhaps destroyed by the winter weather.

Find out more about the story of the Ice Man on pages 10–13.

As the ice melted, more of the Ice Man's body could be seen lying in the rocks where he died. The injury on the back of the head made the police think he was a murder victim, but it was made by an animal sometime after he had died. ▼

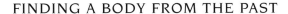

A Body Preserved in a Bog

Lindow Man (see pages 8–9 and 22–24) was found in a peat bog in Cheshire, England, in 1984. The peat, which is used to burn as fuel or to spread on gardens, was being dug out by big machines and turned out onto a conveyor belt to go to a factory.

The workers must have been horrified when they saw a human foot among the peat on the conveyor belt! Only the upper part of Lindow Man's body was still in place in the peat bog. The police thought that it was the body of a recent murder victim, but archaeologists eventually convinced the police that the man had been killed about two thousand years ago.

The well-preserved body of Lindow Man. The peat bog stained his skin dark brown. A fingernail is lying on his chest. ▼

Bodies vs. Bones

Finds like these, in such good condition after hundreds or even thousands of years, are very unusual. Archaeologists can find out much more from a body than from just a skeleton. They can study the contents of the stomach to find out what the person ate for a last meal and see the hair color and the style of dress. Clothes may be preserved too. But the most exciting thing is that we can see—almost face-to-face—these people who lived so long ago.

How Ancient Bodies Were Preserved

The survival of an ancient body, including its bones as well as its internal organs and hair, depends on the ground in which it is lying and on the climate of the country. Bodies are preserved in frozen ground, in hot, dry ground, or in very wet ground, such as peat bogs.

The Big Freeze

Just as a freezer keeps food frozen and stops it from rotting, ice in the ground can also preserve bodies. The bodies of three members of the Franklin Expedition to the Arctic (1845–48), who died in 1846, were buried in deep graves dug in frozen ground (see pages 40–43). Because the Arctic region's summer sun only thaws the surface of the ground, the bodies were found in 1984, still frozen, looking much the same as when they were buried in the mid-nineteenth century.

Natural Mummies

In the hot, dry ground of the American southwest, bodies of Native Americans were buried in pits in caves. These people were known as Basket Makers (see pages 32–35). The bodies slowly dried out, becoming naturally mummified. The fine baskets buried with them were preserved too, although these would have rotted away in damp ground.

◄ Natural mummification is caused by dry heat. This mummy dates back to 3000 B.C. and was found in a desert tomb. It is on display at the British Museum, London.

This is a tree coffin found at Egtved, Denmark. The remains of the body and clothing date back to 1200 B.C. ▼

Careful Ceremony—Mummifying Bodies

In many countries, bodies have been deliberately preserved by drying them in the sun's heat or by the smoke from a fire. In ancient Egypt, embalmers mummified bodies by making a cut in the side and taking out the soft internal organs. The brain was also removed. A chemical called natron was packed around the body to absorb the moisture in it. Finally the body was wrapped in linen bandages and placed in an elaborately decorated coffin.

Tree Coffin Burials

In Denmark three thousand years ago, people were buried in hollowed-out tree-trunk coffins covered by a barrow, or burial mound. In some of these, rainwater seeped into the tree coffin and kept out air and the bacteria that cause decay. Water gushed out when the mounds were dug up later. The water had preserved the bodies and their clothes. (See pages 18–20.)

What We Can Find Out from Ancient Bodies

Why Archaeologists Study Ancient Bodies

Archaeologists find out much more about ancient people from their bodies than from their bones. If skin is preserved, they look for tattoos. The Ice Man had tattoos on his back, knee, and ankle, showing that people decorated their bodies five thousand years ago. The Romans wrote that the Britons painted themselves blue with a dye called woad, which may have meant that they were tattooed. But Lindow Man of Britain was not tattooed. This custom may have become fashionable after his time, since he lived five hundred years or so before the Romans came to Britain.

Inside stomachs there may be traces of the person's last meal. The muddy sludge from the stomachs of the "bog-bodies" of northern Europe (see pages 21–24) was examined under microscopes. The last meal of Tollund Man, found in Denmark, was a porridge made from barley. Seeds of many weeds were also found in the porridge. Botanists, scientists who study plants, have identified the weeds, including linseed and knotweed, as plants that were growing at the time when Tollund Man was alive.

▲ Part of an animal design tattoo along the right arm of a Scythian chief at Pazyryk, in Siberia, Russia. Buried in a deep shaft about 2,400 years ago, water seeped into the tomb and froze, preserving the body with its tattooed skin.

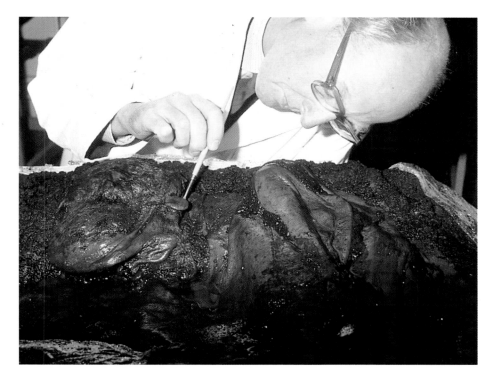

◄ Revealing the face of Lindow Man in a laboratory at the British Museum, London. The peat was sprayed, then carefully loosened and removed with a paintbrush.

The most important information from ancient bodies concerns diseases. These can be identified even in dried-up mummies. Only certain diseases leave traces on bones. Many more can be found in the internal organs and tissues of the body. Egyptian mummies show that many diseases that people suffer from today were present over four thousand years ago. Ancient Egyptians suffered from cancers and lung diseases such as silicosis (caused by breathing in dust or sand).

This information is very useful to doctors who are studying the history of diseases. They want to know how long ago people began to suffer from them, and in what parts of the world the diseases were found. Archaeologists are helping in medical research that may one day lead to the end of some diseases.

The Ice Man

Discovered by chance in a glacier in the Alps (see page 4), the body known as the Ice Man is already providing many clues to life five thousand years ago.

When the body was examined by archaeologists, they found that he was 25 to 35 years old when he died. Evidence shows that he had probably been caught in a storm and took shelter in a hollow at the side of a glacier. He may have fallen asleep and frozen to death.

There was no sign of any wound or disease. The examination also showed he had dark brown curly hair, cut to a length of four inches. He was fairly short, standing just over five feet tall. He would have weighed about 110 pounds. If he had worn modern clothes, he would not have looked very different from someone living in the Alps today.

The face of the Ice Man has been recreated by John Gurche at the Denver Museum of Natural History. He used measurements, X-ray and CAT scans, and three-dimensional computer images. In this way, Gurche was able to make a model of the Ice Man's skull, which gives clues to the muscles and features of the face. Gurche modeled this face over the skull.

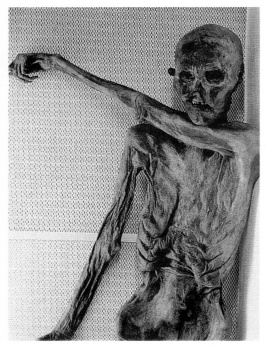

▲ The Ice Man died lying with his arms stretched out in front. But the ice that formed above him moved and turned the body over to lie on its face and moved the arms into this uncomfortable-looking position.

The Ice Man's face was probably damaged by ice moving the body over the rocks. ▶

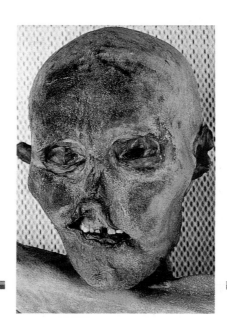

The Ice Man's Clothes and Weapons

When the Ice Man died, he was wearing a leather tunic and pants. Archaeologists pieced the tunic together from over one hundred fragments. His clothing was made of a patchwork of small pieces of sheep or goat skin sewn together with neat stitches of animal sinew or plant thread. It had been repaired rather badly.

Around his shoulders the Ice Man wore a cape made of woven grass. Capes like this were worn out of doors by people in the Alps as recently as a hundred years ago. His shoes were made of leather and stuffed with dried grass to keep his feet warm. A fur cap was also found.

The Ice Man carried a leather backpack with a wooden frame. This is the oldest rucksack in the world. In a deerskin quiver were arrows made from viburnum and dogwood branches. Only two were ready to use, with feathered ends and stone tips. He must have broken his bow, since he had cut some yew wood and had begun to shape it into a new bow. He carried a ball of animal sinew to use as a bowstring.

This is an artist's impression of how the Ice Man may have looked while traveling through the Alps five thousand years ago. ▶

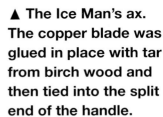

▲ The Ice Man's ax. The copper blade was glued in place with tar from birch wood and then tied into the split end of the handle.

◄ In the center of this photograph you can see the bow that the Ice Man had started to make. It was broken when the body was dug up. Above this are unfinished arrows. Below is the leather quiver and completed arrows.

His flint knife had a wooden handle. Another of his tools was made from a deer antler and would have been used to shape flint arrowheads. A net made of grass cords helped him to catch birds for food. For chopping wood and meat, he carried an ax with a copper blade.

Learning the Ice Man's Secrets

When the body was taken to Innsbruck, Austria, the first task was to preserve it. It was washed in fungicide—special chemicals that stop molds from growing—and kept frozen. Scientists from different parts of the world will perform tests on the body for many years to come.

One of the earliest tests carried out on the Ice Man's body was radiocarbon dating. Pieces of skin and bone were sent to laboratories in Zurich, Switzerland, and Oxford, England, to be dated by the radiocarbon in them. These dates showed that he lived just over five thousand years ago.

The Ice Man's brain and internal organs, such as the stomach, were preserved. It is interesting to compare these with organs of modern people. Scientists are carrying out tests to try to identify the Ice Man's genetic makeup to see if it is possible to link him to a particular group of people, such as the Celts.

▲ Scientists examining the body of the Ice Man

The wooden handles of the Ice Man's tools and the charcoal he was carrying to make a fire have been examined under microscopes to see what trees were growing at that time, and which were used for the ax handle.

An Australian scientist found hairs of ibex and chamois (types of wild goat) and red deer on the blades of the Ice Man's tools, showing which animals he had hunted.

There were also traces of porridge on the ax. Apparently the Ice Man had been eating porridge with his fingers while he was binding his axhead onto the handle. Freezing preserved these traces of his last meal.

Looking inside an Egyptian Mummy

Natsef-Amun was a priest of the sun god Amun in the great temple at Thebes, in Egypt. He died during the reign of King Ramses XI (1113–1085 B.C.) and was buried in a cemetery near the temple.

Examining a Mummy

His mummy was not excavated by archaeologists. Like many others, it was dug up by people looking for mummies to sell. In the nineteenth century, hundreds of tombs were opened. Natsef-Amun's mummy was sent to England and bought in London, then presented to a museum in Leeds.

In 1824, Natsef-Amun's mummy was used for the first scientific examination of a mummy. The mummy was unwrapped and examined by surgeons; a chemist who studied the substances used to preserve the body; an artist who made clear drawings; and people who could read the hieroglyphic inscriptions on the coffin.

In 1989, Natsef-Amun was sent to Manchester Museum in England to be examined again using new technology. The museum has been the center for the Mummy Research Project since 1973. An international Mummy Database has been set up to record information about diseases found in mummies and to supply data to researchers.

▲ The face of Natsef-Amun's mummy. The mouth is open and the tongue is sticking out. Was he strangled?

See page 16.

New Technology

Two recently developed pieces of medical equipment now enable archaeologists to look inside mummies without unwrapping the bandages. The first is the CAT (computerized axial tomography) scanner, which uses X rays to give images of sections of a body from head to foot, like the slices in a loaf of bread.

The second piece of equipment is the flexible endoscope, which is a tube, one tenth of an inch wide, with a television or video camera on the end. Very fine strands of glass send light into the body, and the part of the body being examined is shown on a video monitor screen. In mummies, it can be inserted up the nose into the inside of the skull, where some of the brain may have been left behind when it was extracted by the embalmers.

Different views of the head of an Egyptian girl mummy. The mummy was not unwrapped. These pictures were made by a computer from CAT X-ray data. ▼

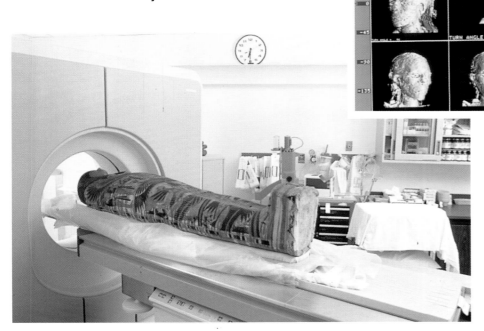

◄ An Egyptian mummy inside its case going into a CAT scanner.

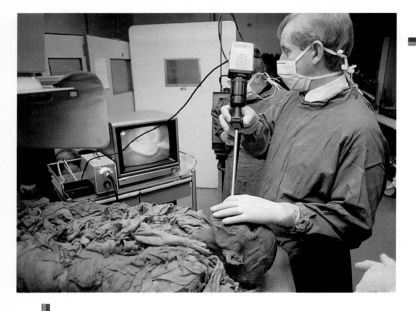

An endoscope can also be inserted through a tiny hole into the body cavity. Most of the internal organs were taken out by the embalmers, but the heart was left, and the chest can be examined to see the ribs and any remains of the lungs. Samples of organs can be taken for analysis in the laboratory.

Was there Foul Play?

One odd feature of Natsef-Amun's body was that his mouth was wide open, with his tongue sticking out, as if he had been strangled. But this would have crushed the windpipe, and the endoscope views down the windpipe, from the mouth and up from the chest, showed that it was undamaged. It may be that Natsef-Amun's tongue was swollen from an insect sting, so he choked to death, but drying the body removed the evidence of swelling.

Reconstructing a Head and Face

Natsef-Amun's face has been restored by Richard Neave, a medical artist at Manchester University. As well as putting faces on ancient skulls, he helps the police by identifying murder victims from skeletons.

Richard Neave needed a model of Natsef-Amun's skull, which could not be made from the fragile mummy. From a CAT scan, information was transferred to a computer screen. This showed a three-dimensional image of the skull. From this, a cutting machine carved a replica of the skull from a block of Styrofoam.

Pieces of toothpicks were put into the replica skull, marking the known thickness of facial muscles and flesh over the bone in different parts. Dummy eyeballs were placed in the eye sockets and eyelids were modeled in clay. Muscles around the mouth and eyes and chewing muscles, which run from the jawbone up the sides of the head, were added. Ears, nose, and lips were shaped, but since these have no bones they cannot be as accurate as the rest of the head.

Since Natsef-Amun's age was known, his face was given a middle-aged look with a wrinkled forehead. The head was left hairless, because Egyptian priests shaved their heads completely.

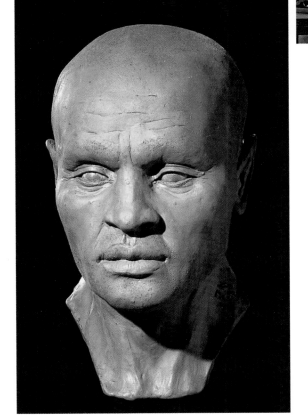

The recontructed head of Natsef-Amun by Richard Neave ▶

▲ Richard Neave starting to reconstruct a face. He carefully applies the clay over the Styrofoam base. The little sticks show the thickness of the facial muscles and mark how much clay to put over the skull.

Bodies in Danish Tree Coffins

▲ This body was found in a tree coffin barrow near Aarhus, Denmark. It is on display in the National Museum, Copenhagen. The hair and eyelashes are not preserved on this body, but they were on many others.

In Denmark, three thousand years ago, men and women were buried fully dressed in coffins made from hollowed-out oak tree trunks. The tree coffin was laid on a bed of big stones, and a mound of turf and stones was heaped over it to make a barrow.

In the nineteenth century, farmers began to dig out the good soil from the rotted turfs to spread on their fields. They opened the tree coffins looking for treasure— usually destroying the burial site. The Danish king Frederick VII was interested in archaeology, and he had one tree coffin carefully opened. Many have now been excavated by archaeologists.

In many barrows there were only a few bones and fragments of cloth. But some barrows had been heaped up on ground where there was a layer of clay. This stopped rainwater from running off into the ground. Instead it seeped into the tree coffin. Inside the coffin, rainwater mixed with an acid chemical called tannin from the oak. This destroyed most of the bones of the body, but preserved the skin, hair, nails, teeth, and the eyelashes. Even the woolen clothes were preserved.

For the burial, a layer of grass was put in the tree coffin, then a cowhide was laid over it, hairy side up. The body was placed on this.

People were buried with their jewelry; women wore bronze earrings and bracelets. Both men and women had wooden or horn combs at their waists, and some had small birch-bark pails of beer or mead. A drinking horn and spoons made of horn were found at some burial sites.

Men were buried with swords or daggers in wooden scabbards. In one tree coffin a small dagger was found in a long sword scabbard. Perhaps a greedy relative kept the dead man's sword! Folding stools, one with a seat of otter skin, were also found.

Lengths of woolen cloth were cut up and wrapped around the feet of the body and under the head as a pillow. Some were laid over the body. One piece found in a coffin told scientists about the width of the loom on which it was woven. There were three finished edges. The two side edges showed that the cloth was over six feet wide.

Finally the sides of the cowhide were brought up to cover the body, and the heavy lid was put on.

▲ This photograph shows a tree coffin on its layer of stones. It was found when a barrow was dug out at Egtved, Denmark. (See pages 7 and 20.)

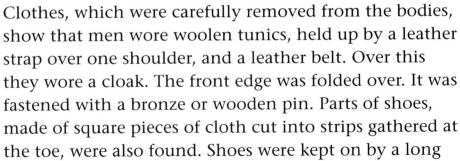

The inside of a tree coffin found at Egtved. You can see the covering cloth on the right and the cowhide underneath. The clothing, hair, and jewelry are still in place. ▼

Clothes, which were carefully removed from the bodies, show that men wore woolen tunics, held up by a leather strap over one shoulder, and a leather belt. Over this they wore a cloak. The front edge was folded over. It was fastened with a bronze or wooden pin. Parts of shoes, made of square pieces of cloth cut into strips gathered at the toe, were also found. Shoes were kept on by a long leather strip tied around the foot. Strips of cloth were tied around the ankle to keep the shoe from rubbing.

Women wore shirts made from a single piece of cloth with a hole cut for the head. One edge was folded over to make sleeves, which were stitched under the arm. The sides of the cloth were joined across the back. Women wore small hair nets made of horsehair or thicker braided caps that tied under the chin or at the back. One elaborate braided headdress was made by the technique called "sprang," which is still used today in Denmark.

All the men were clean-shaven—no traces were found of beards or mustaches. Small bronze blades found buried with men were probably their razors.

Bog Bodies of Northern Europe

In May, 1950, Professor Peter Glob, a Danish archaeologist, was lecturing to his university students at Aarhus, Denmark. There was a knock at the door, and he was asked to go to the telephone to speak to the police. The police asked him to look at a body found by workers cutting peat. Professor Glob set off at once to a small peat bog in the hills of Jutland. There he saw, eight or nine feet down, in the peat-diggers' trench, the shoulder and foot of a human body sticking out of the ground. Professor Glob dug carefully to remove peat from the shoulder area and revealed the man's head. "As dusk fell," he wrote later, "we saw in the fading light a man take shape before us. He was curled up, with legs drawn up under and arms bent, resting on his side as if asleep." But the man had not died in his sleep. He had been hanged with a braided leather rope that was still around his neck. This find was named Tollund Man, after the area where he was found.

Professor Glob had the body dug out in a lump of peat. It was taken quickly to the National Museum at Copenhagen before exposure to air made it decay. Preserving bodies to display in a museum is such a slow and expensive process that only the head of Tollund Man was preserved.

The peaceful face of Tollund Man. A noose of braided leather is around his neck— does this mean there had been foul play? Find out on page 24. ▼

How Peat Preserves

The preserved body of Grauballe Man is on display in Aarhus Museum, Denmark. ▼

Over one thousand bodies have been found preserved in peat bogs in northern Germany, Scandinavia, and the British Isles. Peat forms from the remains of slowly decaying plants. The bodies were thrown into pools containing sphagnum moss. An acid in this moss tanned the skin like leather, which preserved it and turned it dark brown. We can now see the faces of people who lived about two thousand years ago. Scientists can tell how old they were when they died and examine the stomach and intestines to see what they ate for their last meals.

Grauballe Man

In 1952, Professor Glob studied another bog body, Grauballe Man. This find was dramatic because his throat had been cut from ear to ear. His whole body was preserved by keeping it first in water, then replacing the water with oils and letting it slowly dry out.

Preserving bog bodies is a difficult task. Lindow Man (see page 5) was found in England, in 1984. His body was preserved in the British Museum by the then new technique of freeze-drying. While the body was being studied, it was kept in a freezer and could only be worked on for short periods to prevent it from decaying in the air.

What They Ate

Examination of these bodies shows what life was like two thousand years ago. Lindow Man's hands and fingernails were very well-kept, showing he had not done manual work. Perhaps he was a chief. The food in his stomach was unleavened bread, made without yeast.

Fragments of bone in Grauballe Man's stomach showed that he ate meat. There were also millions of eggs of intestinal worms in his stomach, which live in badly cooked meat. These have been found in many other bog bodies.

How They Died

Sometimes archaeologists can find out the ways in which these people died. The body of a 14-year-old girl was found at Domlandsmoor, northern Germany. One side of her head was shaved, and she had been blindfolded—the bandage was still around her eyes.

Roman writers recorded that among the people of this area, the punishment of an unfaithful wife was to be drowned in a lake after her head had been shaved. This may have been the fate of this girl— and would show that girls married very young.

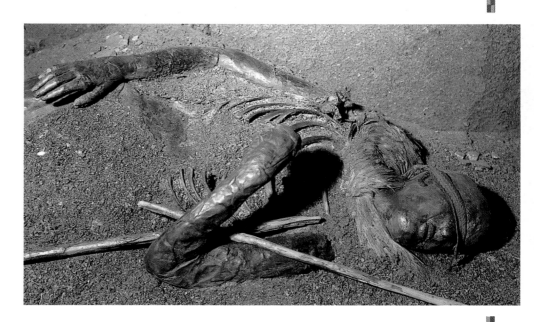

The body of a blindfolded girl found at Domlandsmoor, northern Germany. She was 14 years old when she died. ▼

Sacrifice to the Gods?

The men from Tollund, Grauballe, and Lindow may not have been murdered but killed as sacrifices to gods or goddesses, perhaps in the hope of making crops grow well. The Tollund and Grauballe men had eaten ergot, a grain fungus that acts as a narcotic. They might have been made unconscious before they were put to death. They were naked, which may have been part of a ceremony. Tollund Man was hanged. This was probably an honorable form of death. In Viking times, a hanged man was thought to go to live with the god Odin.

▲ Tollund Man as the body was found by Professor Glob in 1950. The picture shows the noose around his neck.

Lindow Man died in a violent way. He was hit on the head with an ax, making a hole in his skull. The jugular vein in his neck was cut, so, like Grauballe Man, he would have bled a lot. Finally, he was strangled with a thin cord that was still tied around his neck when he was found.

These men, along with similar finds, may have been the victims of sacrifices, perhaps linked with the fertility of the fields. The face of Tollund Man is peaceful. In many lands, victims, even chiefs, were content to be sacrificed if they believed it would help their people to survive.

The Jade Burial Suits

In July 1968, a wonderful tomb was discovered at Mancheng, about 90 miles south of Beijing in China. Workers were digging on the side of a hill, when suddenly the ground opened up under their feet! They had broken through the roof of an ancient burial chamber. Archaeologists were told of the find and came to excavate the tomb. They found that it was the tomb of a prince. Inscriptions on objects in the tomb identified him as Liu Sheng, a prince of the Han dynasty.

Soon afterward another tomb was found nearby, the tomb of Liu's wife, the princess Tou Wan, who died in 120 B.C. Each tomb was over 160 feet long, consisting of several rooms hacked out of solid rock.

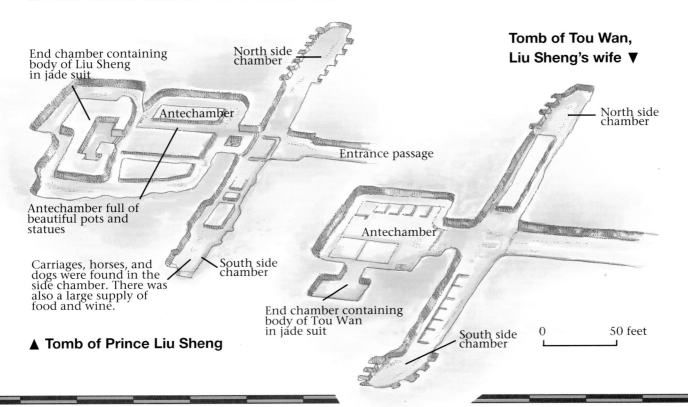

End chamber containing body of Liu Sheng in jade suit

North side chamber

Antechamber

Antechamber full of beautiful pots and statues

Carriages, horses, and dogs were found in the side chamber. There was also a large supply of food and wine.

South side chamber

▲ **Tomb of Prince Liu Sheng**

Tomb of Tou Wan, Liu Sheng's wife ▼

North side chamber

Entrance passage

Antechamber

End chamber containing body of Tou Wan in jade suit

South side chamber

0   50 feet

Tou Wan's tomb was more difficult to enter. The entrance was blocked not only with large stones, but with a barrier of iron. The iron had been melted and poured into the opening and left to become solid. In the end, soldiers were called in to help. They carefully dynamited their way in.

These leopards are made of gilded bronze inlaid with silver and garnets. They are only one and a half inches high. There were four found, and they were probably used to hold down the corners of the cloth covering Tou Wan's body. ▼

A Precious Find

Archaeologists are often disappointed when they find the burial site of an important person. All over the world, tomb robbers have taken the precious things left with the dead. No robbers had broken into these two tombs. Nearly three thousand wonderful objects of jade (a greenish white stone) and bronze were inside. The vases, acupuncture needles, lamps, and weapons were for the use of the prince and princess in the afterlife. The bronze objects have revealed a lot about how craftspeople worked at that time and have shown the beauty of the lamps and many other things that they made.

Magical Suits

The most exciting discoveries were the suits of jade in which the bodies had been dressed. Each suit was made of over two thousand thin plaques of jade. The plaques measured 1.8 x 1.4 inches to .6 x .4 inches. They were .08 to .14 inches thick. A tiny hole was drilled in each corner, except on the chest pieces, where the plaques were glued to a cloth lining. Gold thread was used to join the plaques together. Each suit was in twelve separate pieces for the hands, feet, head, body, arms, and legs. Each part was bound at the edges with iron wire covered with silk.

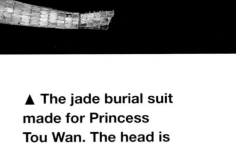

▲ **The jade burial suit made for Princess Tou Wan. The head is resting on a stone pillow.**

Suits like these were described by Chinese writers, but these were the only complete ones to be found. The gold thread had rotted, but archaeologists could see exactly how the suits were made. Jade was the most precious of all materials in China. The Chinese believed that a piece of jade placed near a body would preserve it forever. The prince and princess had whole suits made for themselves. But the magic didn't work. Archaeologists found only a little dust among the jade plaques. The bodies had completely decayed.

The plaques of jade were pieced together in sections and then the sections were fitted together around the body. ▶

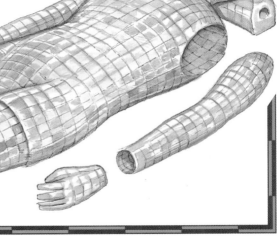

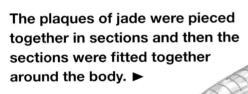

The Plaster People of Pompeii

Pompeii was a busy country town on the shores of the Bay of Naples, in Italy. One morning in A.D. 79 there was a terrifying explosion. The volcano Vesuvius, five miles away, erupted and a huge cloud of ash blotted out the sun and began to fall on the town.

Most people rushed out into the countryside as the roofs of houses collapsed under the weight of ash. Those who stopped to collect their valuables or decided to guard their homes were poisoned by fumes or suffocated by the ash.

Fiorelli's Discovery

Pompeii was buried under a blanket of ash and the town was abandoned until the eighteenth century. Then parts of the town were dug up by people looking for statues and other things to sell. In 1860, Giuseppe Fiorelli was put in charge. Fiorelli was the first archaeologist at Pompeii to write down where finds were uncovered and make a plan of the buried town. Also, he found the bodies of some of the people who had lived there.

◄ This man died when the volcano Vesuvius, in the background, erupted. His skull is showing through the plaster cast that has preserved the shape of his body.

Rising from the Ashes

Ash covered the bodies and became hard. The bodies rotted away, leaving only a hollow space and some bones. The plaster-cast "bodies" were recreated by pouring plaster into the hollow space. When the plaster set, the hard ash was carefully scraped away. The shape of a human body, looking like a statue, was revealed.

This plaster cast is thought to be of a beggar's body. It shows that he died holding a cloth to his mouth to breathe through, but he was still suffocated by the volcanic ash. ▶

During the eruption, some people took shelter in cellars and rooms that were not filled with ash. They were found as skeletons. But the "statue" bodies (see above) show what the people of Pompeii looked like. Their faces are almost lifelike. Some are old, some young.

We can see how people died. Some had pulled up their clothes over their faces in order to keep out the ash and try to breathe. Some were struggling to get up. One man died as he tried to pull his goat along. The bodies of many dogs were found, still chained up at house doors.

Thanks to Fiorelli's careful work, the casts of many of the people of Pompeii can still be seen in the museum there. They show the horror of that dreadful summer day nearly two thousand years ago.

The Paracas Mummies of Peru

Two important burial sites with mummies were found in the 1920s in Peru by Dr. Julio C. Tello, a Peruvian archaeologist. One burial site was for ordinary people and contained the bodies of men, women, and children. The other was only for older men, who may have been priests. These people lived long before the Incas established their great Empire in South America.

The sites were found on the dry sandy coast, on the Paracas peninsula, 125 miles south of Lima, the capital of Peru. The bodies were not treated with special substances. The soft insides were removed, and the bodies dried out in the sand naturally.

Buried in Baskets

What makes these cemeteries remarkable is that the dead were buried with fabric, much of which was perfectly preserved in the dry sand. When a person died, the naked body was placed sitting in a basket, to make it as small as possible. Then large cotton cloths were wound around the body and basket until the conical bundle was about five feet high and the same across the base.

A simplified diagram of a Paracas mummy from inside a bundle. There were usually up to 23 layers of wrapping. The legs were drawn up and the arms were bent, with the hands around the face, to make the body as small as possible. ▼

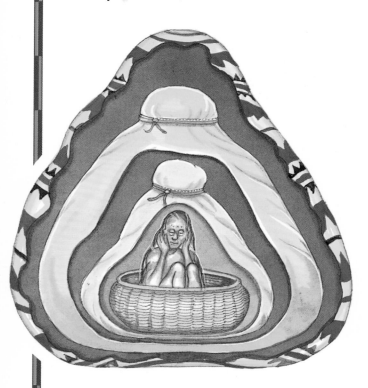

As the cloths were wound around, all sorts of things were wrapped in them: gold nose-rings, shell necklaces, weapons, and pots. Sometimes the bodies of pet animals were put in as well as food. Some people were buried with 150 of these offerings.

The food from mummy bundles shows that the people were farmers. They grew corn, cassava, sweet potatoes, beans, and peanuts.

Beautiful Textiles

Men wore loincloths, skirts, headdresses, short capes, and large cloaks. The textiles were woven from cotton and from the wool of animals such as llamas—there were no sheep in Peru. Some were fine gauze, while others were heavy materials decorated with colorful stitching. Clothes had stitched designs of cats, fish, birds, and other creatures. The beautiful soft colors were made from vegetable dyes—red, pink, yellow, blue, green, and brown. These materials are remarkable for the skill with which they were woven and embroidered and that so many have been preserved after being buried for two thousand years.

◄ **A dancing man embroidered on clothing found in a Paracas mummy.**

A model wearing the beautifully decorated garments buried in a Paracas mummy bundle. ▼

The Basket Makers of the Southwest

Around 1917, American archaeologists were exploring part of Arizona, looking for caves. This land is desert, with steep gorges between weathered rocks. The archaeologists were clambering along ledges high above the valley floor when they spotted above them the mouth of an enormous cave with an entrance over forty yards wide. They found later that it could not be seen at all from the valley below. They had to scramble up a steep slope for one hundred feet before they could get into the cave.

Mummies in the Caves

When they excavated the cave they found deep pits where men, women, and children were buried. Because of the lack of rain in Arizona, the bodies had dried out and were naturally mummified. Clothes, food, and many baskets were discovered in the graves.

◀ **The red outline shows the homeland of the Basket Makers.**

White Dog Cave

The first thing the excavators uncovered in one grave was a round basket with a big carrying basket beside it. Underneath the carrying basket were three basket work trays. They lifted these up and saw long white hairs. This was the mummy of a dog with long white fur. This is why the cave has been named "White Dog Cave." We do not know what the Basket Makers themselves called it.

The dog had been buried some time after it died, because there had been time for flies to lay eggs on its body. The flies hatched after the dog was buried and could not escape from the grave. Lots of dead flies were found around the dog. The dog was buried beside its master, a man about 35 years old. The man was lying curled up on his left side, wrapped in a cloth. The baskets had been carefully placed over the body, to protect it when sand was thrown into the grave.

Beside the man's grave was another pit, in which a woman was buried lying on her right side. The lower part of her body had been put into a large woven bag, and another one had been put over her head down to the waist. The bags were sewn together with thread made from the yucca plant. Her body was protected by baskets. Grass seeds, nuts, and squash seeds were found in some of them. Her little dog was buried with her. Its body was lying on a thick bed of fur and feathers. Pointed digging sticks for breaking up the ground were buried with her to help her to grow crops in the afterlife.

Baskets covering the grave of a man and his white dog ▼

33

Basket Makers

Instead of making clay pots, these Native Americans made baskets of all shapes and sizes. They have become known as the Basket Makers. The baskets were made by coiling thin twigs with soft, pithy centers and fixing the coils together with fibers made from yucca leaves. For carrying water, carrier baskets were shaped to be worn on the back. The top of the basket was curved inward, so water did not splash out. The inside was waterproofed with gum from the piñon tree. Today, the descendants of these people still make baskets, which are now sold to tourists. The women who make them draw the fibers through their teeth to make them pliable (soft). This scratches the teeth. Identical scratches are found on the teeth of the ancient Basket Makers.

▲ A basket for carrying water. It would be strapped to a person's back with material that passed through the handles on the sides (now broken).

Hairstyles

Because of the dry ground, hair was preserved, showing styles of hairdressing.

A scalp was found buried with one man. Perhaps it was the head of an enemy he had killed. It had a loop so it could be hung up. The scalp was made by removing the skin from the whole head. It was then dried, stuffed, and sewn up with tiny stitches.

The man who was scalped wore his hair long. A strip up the middle of his head was shaved, running up to a shaved area on the top of his head. This was painted greenish-white, and there was a streak of yellow across the forehead. His face was painted red and white.

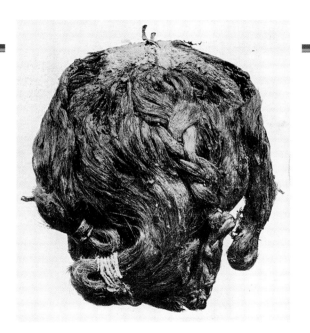

◄ The back view of a scalp showing the braided hair at the back and sides

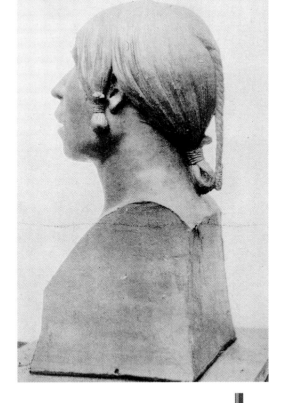

This is what the hairstyle would have looked like. ►

The long hair on each side was brought up and tied in loops over the ears, and the hair at the back was also looped up.

Sandals

As well as baskets, these people wove different kinds of sandals, which were found on the feet of the dead. The most hard-wearing were woven from yucca fibers. Sandals made from cedar bark were softer to wear but wore out more quickly. Mountain sheep hide was also used, with a toe loop over the second and third toes and a loop around the heel made of human hair.

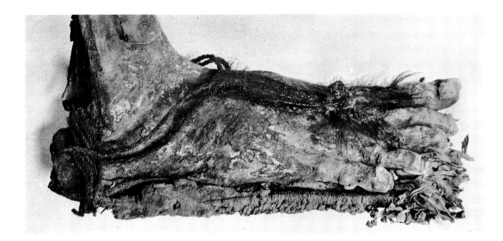

◄ This photograph shows a Basket Maker's mummified foot still wearing a woven sandal.

The Spitalfields Bodies

When archaeologists examine a body, they want to find out how old the person was when he or she died. The age of the person at death can tell us a lot about that person's culture. For example, when life had more hardships, people died at a younger age. Someone who was forty might be considered old in that culture.

From the study of many skeletons, archaeologists have worked out a number of clues from bones that help them to say how old the person was when he or she died. It is important that archaeologists can check the ways in which they work out people's age from remains. This is why the bodies from the vaults under Christ Church, Spitalfields, in London, have been very important to archaeologists.

An open coffin and its occupant from the Spitalfields vaults. The burial garments, pillow, and shroud (the cloth that covers a dead body), are amazingly well-preserved. ▼

The Finds in the Vaults

The remains in the Spitalfields vaults are the bodies of people who were buried between 1729 and 1852. At this time, people were terrified that their bodies would be dug up from graves in churchyards and sold to hospitals for medical

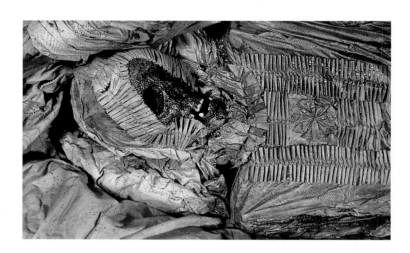

students to cut up to practice surgical operations. Many people paid extra money to be buried under the church.

In 1981, church authorities asked archaeologists to examine the bodies and have them taken out to be cremated. Between 1984 and 1986 about one thousand bodies were moved. Some were well preserved. Many were skeletons, while others were mummified, dried out by drafts blowing through the passages between the vaults. There was a danger that germs of fatal diseases such as smallpox might still be alive in the bodies. Archaeologists were inoculated and wore special clothing, including masks, for safety. They worked in choking dust, with dim light and no heat in winter.

Aging Remains

Each coffin had a name and date so scientists knew the exact ages of the bodies. This is how the archaeologists were able to test the latest way of aging skeletons. It is called the Complex Method. It relies on examining changes in the skull, pelvis, and the long bones of the arms and the legs as a person gets older. The archaeologists used these clues to age a body. Then they looked at the age on the coffin lid to see if they were right.

Archaeologists found that by using the Complex Method, people of seventy appeared younger than that. On other excavations, therefore, they had been miscalculating when people died. These people had lived longer than previously believed.

▲ This is one of the beautifully engraved coffin plates that had a name, age, and date of death. This information helped the scientists decide if the Complex Method worked or not.

Useful evidence has also been found on the teeth of children. The length of developing molars can now be linked with exact ages of children. This evidence will be used on digs where there is no written evidence for the ages of children. It is being used now to find the ages of Neanderthal children who lived about thirty thousand years ago. It is possible that the teeth developed at slightly different ages in this different kind of human, but the new calculations will give a better guide.

The examination of the bodies in Spitalfields gives clues to diet and life in the eighteenth and nineteenth centuries. Many bones contained large amounts of zinc and copper, which are found in oysters. Although oysters are now very expensive, they were cheap at that time. Millions were eaten in England every year, and the remains in the vaults bear this out.

Many bones also contained lead. This came from drinking water stored in lead tanks and also from lead put into food by cheating shopkeepers to make it weigh more. The lead gradually poisoned people.

The skull of a person who committed suicide clearly shows the bullet wound. ▼

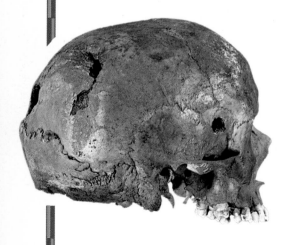

Other Discoveries in the Vaults

There was evidence about the work of dentists in the eighteenth century. Several people had dental plates with false teeth. Some were recycled teeth, taken from bodies in graves or on battlefields. The dental plates were usually made of gold.

One man suffered so terribly from toothaches and from the pain of gout in his feet it seems he shot himself. The hole made by the bullet can be seen on the skull.

Today many older people, mainly women, suffer from osteoporosis, a disease that makes their bones become brittle and break easily. Among the Spitalfields women few had developed brittle bones. Perhaps this was because they walked everywhere, since there were no cars. The exercise and their healthy diet of fish and oysters made their skeletons look much younger than the writing on the coffin lids said they were.

Many children suffered from a disease called rickets. Their bones did not contain enough calcium and grew curved instead of straight. This disease is also caused by lack of vitamin D, which comes mainly from sunshine. We know from records that the nineteenth century was a time of cold summers and long winters. Rickets was also caused by bad diet. Very young children were fed on cereal mixed with water. Because they did not get enough milk, meat, and fresh vegetables, they lacked the vitamins and minerals that would enable their bones to grow properly.

The work at Spitalfields has shown archaeologists the inaccuracy of current methods of aging bodies.

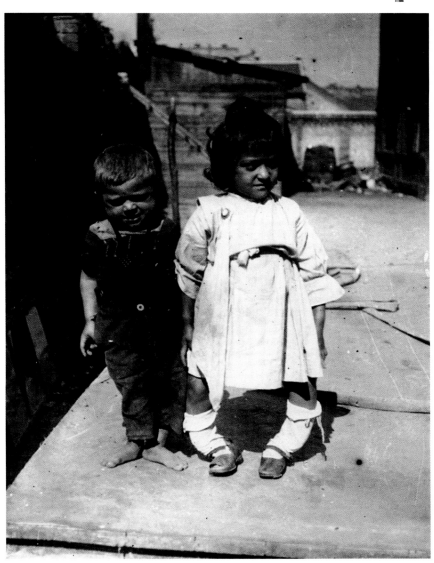

▲ The disease rickets causes the bones to grow out of shape.

The Tragic Franklin Expedition

"**H**e's there, he's right there!" gasped archaeologist Arne Carlson. In 1984, as warm water melted the ice in the coffin of a Victorian sailor, Carlson was able to lift a piece of cloth that covered his face.

The buried sailor was a member of Sir John Franklin's expedition that had sailed from London in May 1845. The team was looking for the Northwest Passage, a way to go from east to west along the northern coasts of the American continent. The ship never returned, and all 125 men and 4 cabin boys aboard, with their dog Neptune and their monkey Jacko, died in the frozen wastes of the Arctic.

A map showing the area where the Franklin Expedition came to its end.

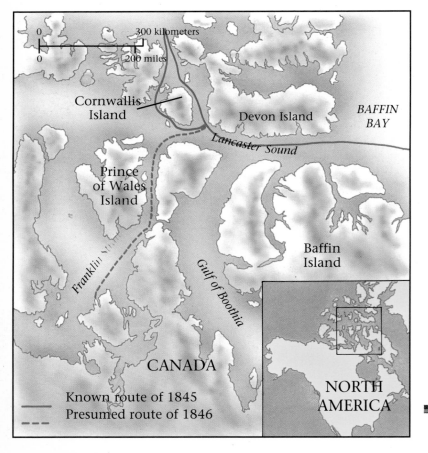

In 1850, a rescue expedition found the site where Franklin had set up a camp on Beechey Island, as his ships were stuck all winter in the frozen sea. The graves of three men who had died there were also found. Another expedition, far to the south on King William Island, found a message in a pile of rough stones, saying that Franklin and many men had died. The survivors were abandoning the ships, which had been frozen in the ice for 19 months, and were going to walk south across the frozen sea to the mainland.

In 1879, an American expedition discovered the fate of these men. They had reached the mainland only to die at Starvation Cove, where their bones were found.

The Search for Clues to the Mystery

It was a mystery why the well-equipped expedition had come to such a terrible end. In 1984, Professor Owen Beattie of the University of Edmonton, Canada, led an expedition to Beechey Island to examine the bodies of the three men buried there. If their bodies were well-preserved by freezing, he could find out why they had died. This could give clues to the failure of the whole expedition.

A Kettle and the First Body

Although it was summer, the excavation of the first grave, that of John Torrington, was difficult because the ground remained frozen. It had to be melted with hot water before the archaeologists could dig. At last the coffin was revealed. After burial, water had seeped into the coffin, and the body was set in ice. This was melted with warm water until the body could be lifted out and examined.

▲ Professor Beattie went back to Beechey Island in 1986 to investigate two more graves. This is the grave of John Hartnell.

John Torrington's body was perfectly preserved. He had medium-brown hair and was five feet five inches tall. He was wearing linen pants and a blue-and-white striped shirt.

Beattie wore double surgical gloves to protect him from any diseases that might still be able to harm him. He took samples of the internal organs, the brain, hair, bone, and nails. These were put into sealed containers for study in a laboratory. Beattie had to keep dipping his hands in warm water while he worked on the frozen body. John Torrington had been a stoker, handling dirty coal, but his hands and nails were clean. This showed he had been too sick to work for some time before he died. He had also been too sick to eat—his stomach had no food in it.

In a later expedition, in 1986, the bodies of John Hartnell and William Braine were examined in the same way, and samples were taken. Each body was carefully restored to its coffin and the grave was filled in.

A Clue to the End

Near the graves and camp on Beechey Island, Beattie found a dump of hundreds of food cans. He examined them and saw that the seams were closed with lead solder inside as well as outside. The lead inside the tin can would have contaminated the food and poisoned the people who ate it. Preserving food in cans was still a very new method at the time of the expedition. Perhaps Franklin and his men had died from lead poisoning.

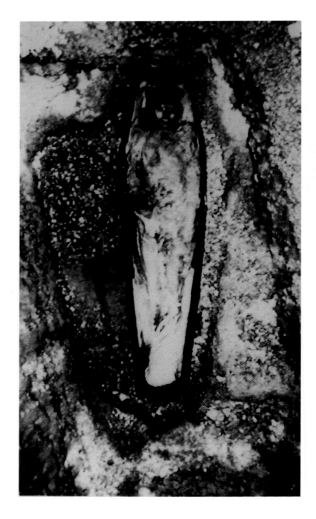

▲ The body of John Hartnell preserved by ice in the coffin

Lead poisoning makes people weak and affects the nervous system so they cannot think properly. Often they do peculiar things. As the crew ate more and more of the canned food, the officers might have made bad decisions. One rescue expedition found a lifeboat that men had filled with things from the ships, when they set out for land. The only food was tea and chocolate. They had put in books, handkerchiefs, toothbrushes, soap, and slippers, useless items for the trek to the mainland. It looked as though the men had been too sick to plan clearly for their survival.

▲ Relics left at Starvation Cove by members of the crew. In 1878, a U.S. rescue expedition led by Frederick Schwatka met Inuit who had found the items.

Beattie sent samples from the three dead men to a laboratory to find out how much lead there was in them. There was many times the normal amount. The evidence from hair was especially important. Because hair grows quickly, the lead in the newer hair growth proved that the men had not been poisoned in England, but during the voyage.

Rest in Peace?

Many people think that bodies should be left undisturbed where they were buried. But, you can see from reading this book that bodies teach us about the past. We learn what people looked like and what diseases they had. Bodies even solve mysteries, such as the fate of the Franklin Expedition. So, this important work contributes a great deal to our knowledge of the past.

Time Line

EUROPE	NEAR EAST

A.D.

1984 – 86 Excavations at Christ Church, Spitalfields, London.

1984 Lindow Man found in England.

1950 Professor Glob found Tollund Man and Grauballe Man in 1952, in Denmark.

1860 Fiorelli creates plaster-cast bodies at Pompeii, Italy.

1800s Tree coffins found in Denmark.

1729–1852 Londoners buried in the vaults under Christ Church, Spitalfields.

79 Pompeii buried after the eruption of Vesuvius, Italy.

B.C.

500 Burial of tattooed bodies of Scyths, a group of people from Siberia, Russia.

1200s Bodies buried in oak tree coffins, Denmark.

3000 The Ice Man lived in Austria.

4000 The first farmers came to British Isles with stone tools and clay pots.

6000 Farming began in southeastern Europe.

A.D.
1095–1276 Crusades to the Holy Land.

B.C.
1100 Natsef-Amun died and his body was mummified.

2686–2181 The Old Kingdom in Egypt, when the first pyramids were built.

3000 The first cities in the Near East, with writing, and copper, bronze, and gold in use.

8000–6000 Farming began in Iran, north Iraq, Anatolia, and Syria.

This time line shows how the finds described in each chapter relate to important events in the parts of the world where they were found.

FAR EAST	NORTH AND SOUTH AMERICA

FAR EAST

A.D.
1968 Discovery of the tombs of Liu Sheng and Tou Wan in China.

B.C.
113 Liu Sheng and Tou Wan buried in jade suits at Mancheng, China.

221 First Emperor of China (Chin Dynasty). Great Wall of China built.

400 The Chinese made cast iron.

551 Birth of Chinese sage Confucius.

1500 The Shang dynasty in China. The first cities with writing and bronze-working.

7000 Farming began in north China.

NORTH AND SOUTH AMERICA

A.D.
1984 and 1986 Professor Beattie excavated graves of three men of the Franklin Expedition.

1920s Dr. Tello excavated Paracas cemeteries in Peru and found mummy bundles.

1917 Excavation of the White Dog Cave with the mummies of Basket Makers, Arizona.

1845–1848 The Franklin Expedition. Sir John Franklin and his crew die in the Arctic.

1534 Conquest of the Inca Empire by Spanish.

1400 Rise of the Inca Empire in Peru.

1–700 Basket Makers lived in the American Southwest.

1–200 The people of Paracas, Peru, buried their dead as mummies wrapped in very fine embroidered cloths and clothes.

B.C.
4000 Farming began in Peru.

Glossary

acupuncture A medical treatment in which needles are stuck into certain parts of the body.

afterlife The place where the soul of a dead person is believed, by people in many cultures, to spend the rest of its existence.

Arctic region The area around the North Pole.

bacteria Tiny creatures in water, the ground, and in diseased plants and animals that multiply and feed off decaying matter.

cancer Disease that causes the cells of the body to multiply and spread at an abnormal rate. It damages the body and can lead to death.

CAT scans The images of sections of the inside of a body or organ. They are produced by a machine called a CAT scanner.

Celts Pre-Roman people of central and western Europe whose descendants still live in some areas today.

cremated When a corpse (dead body) is burned as part of a burial ceremony.

embalmers People who treat bodies to preserve them from decay.

flint A hard stone that was often shaped into arrowheads and knives in ancient times.

genetic (makeup) Every cell in the body is made up of genes, which are passed on from parents to child. They pass on characteristics such as eye color. The study of the genetic link between generations is called genetics.

hieroglyphic inscriptions The writing of ancient Egypt, which was made up of symbols.

Incas The people who formed a great empire in Peru, South America, beginning in 1200. The empire was destroyed by the Spanish in 1534.

intestinal worms Worms that live in the intestines of animals and humans, where food is digested.

internal organs The parts of the body, such as the heart, lungs, liver, and stomach, each of which perform a certain function.

microscopes Instruments used to see tiny objects in detail.

mummified When a body has dried out naturally by heat, or after removing soft parts of the body and treating the body with chemicals.

narcotic A drug that can make the body numb to pain or even unconscious.

Neanderthal A group of early humans who lived in much of Europe thousands of years ago.

preserved Protected from decay.

radiocarbon dating A way of dating remains or ancient material by measuring the amount of radioactive carbon in them. This dating method relies on the fact that living things absorb radioactive carbon atoms when alive, but stop absorbing them when they die. The radioactive carbon atoms break down at a steady rate, so by measuring the amount of radiocarbon atoms left in the remains a scientist can work out their age.

sinew The tough tissue that joins muscle to bone. Animal sinew can be used as thick thread.

tattoos Patterns made on the skin using special needles and ink or dye.

X rays Rays that can pass through some parts of the body, or an object, very easily but less easily through other parts. The pictures produced from X rays reveal what lies underneath the surface of an object.

Further Reading

Bendick, Jeanne. *Tombs of the Ancient Americas*. First Books. New York: Franklin Watts, 1993.

Coote, Roger. *The Egyptians*. Look into the Past. New York: Thomson Learning, 1993.

Humphrey, Kathryn Long. *Pompeii: Nightmare at Midday*. First Books. New York: Franklin Watts, 1990.

Martell, Hazel Mary. *The Ancient Chinese*. Worlds of the Past. New York: New Discovery, 1993.

McIntosh, Dr. Jane. *Archeology*. New York: Alfred A. Knopf, 1994.

Putnam, Jim. *Mummy*. New York: Alfred A. Knopf Books for Young Readers, 1993.

Museums

The American Museum of Natural History
Central Park West at 79th Street
New York, NY 10024
(212) 873-1300

The Brooklyn Museum
200 Eastern Parkway
Brooklyn, NY 11238
(718) 638-5000

The Field Museum of Natural History
Roosevelt Road at Lake Shore Drive
Chicago, IL 60605
(312) 922-9410

The Peabody Museum of Archaeology and Ethnology
Harvard University
Cambridge, MA
(617) 495 7535

The University Museum of Archaeology and Anthropology
University of Pennsylvania
33rd and Spruce Streets
Philadelphia, PA 19104
(215) 898-4000

Index